Cast Down
BUT NOT DESTROYED

ONE WOMAN'S STORY OF OVERCOMING ABUSE

SAMANTHA M. PHILLIPS

i

Cast Down But Not Destroyed: One Women's Story of Overcoming Abuse

ISBN: 978-1-934746-09-7

Published by KLIC Publishers Inc., P.O. Box 450097, Kissimmee, Florida 34745

Unless otherwise indicated, all scripture quotations are from the New International Version of the Bible.

DEDICATION

I dedicate this book to my wonderful husband, my hero, Dr Michael A. Phillips.

So many years ago, when God delivered me from abuse, you stepped in and became my Boaz. You proved that real men don't abuse, are faithful and are great fathers. God has used you to heal me, bless me and love me. Over the years, you've always pushed me forward and encouraged me to shine where lesser men would suppress and diminish. For that, I am excessively grateful. I love you!

CONTENTS

Acknowledgments   vii

Foreword   Pg 1

Introduction   Pg 5

1   Where He Found Me   Pg 9

2   How He Touched Me   Pg 41

3   How He Changed Me   Pg 53

4   How He Empowered Me   Pg 67

5   How He Blessed Me   Pg 79

Conclusion of the Matter   Pg 121

ACKNOWLEDGMENTS

I'd like to acknowledge my mentor, Dr Myles Munroe for giving me the charge to press on and get my books completed right away. Thank you for showing me the importance of managing my time well and the priority of my Kingdom assignment. Dr Michael and I are forever grateful for your tutelage.

I'd also like to acknowledge Bishop I.V. & Pastor Bridget Hilliard for teaching and modeling faith like no one else could. Your consistent example of faithfulness and commitment to your marriage and the lifestyle of faith has been a life saving example for me.

I would like to acknowledge both the Orlando Union Rescue Mission and the Soldiers to Scholars Program. God used you as a major part of transforming my life in the beginning of my walk with God. Thank you for your labor of love to serve the underprivileged of our community.

Finally, the staff and leadership team of Kingdom Life International Team Church with special mention to Associate Pastors Erik & Jennifer Enders and Elder Melissa Phillips. Because you all rise to the occasion and put your hands to the plow, we are free to fulfill every part of the mission God has given us. If you weren't doing your jobs, I may not have been able to complete this book.

FOREWARD
By Dr Myles Munroe

This erudite, eloquent, and immensely thought-provoking work gets to the heart of the deepest passions and aspirations of the human heart - to be free from the weights of the past that hinder the manifestation of our divine future. This book is indispensable reading for anyone who wants to overcome the scars of past hurts and live life above the norm. This is a profound authoritative work which expresses the wisdom of the ages and yet breaks new ground in its approach in tackling this sensitive subject and will possibly become a classic in this and the next generation. This exceptional work by Samantha Phillips is one of the most profound, practical, principle-centered approaches to this highly sensitive subject I have read in a long time. The author's approach to this timely issue touches the heart, stirs the emotions and brings a fresh breath of air that captivates the imagination, engages the mind and inspires the spirit of the reader.

The author's ability to leap over complicated theological and metaphysical jargon and reduce complex theories to simple practical principles that the least among us can understand is amazing.

This work will challenge the intellectual while embracing the laymen as it dismantles the mysterious of a soul torn by abuse and hurt and yet delivers solutions that are profound and yet simple. Samantha's approach awakens in the reader the untapped inhibiters that retard our personal development.

The author's personal antidotes and experiences openly exposed in the work empower us to rise above these self-defeating, self-limiting factors to a life of exploits in spiritual and mental advancement. The author also integrates into each chapter the time-tested precepts giving each principle a practical application to life making the entire process people-friendly.

Every sentence of this book is pregnant with wisdom and I enjoyed the mind-expanding

3

experience of this exciting book. I admonish you to
plunge into this ocean of knowledge and watch
your life change for the better.

Dr. Myles Munroe
BFM International
ITWLA
Nassau Bahamas

INTRODUCTION

Thank you for purchasing my debut book, Cast Down But Not Destroyed: One Woman's Story of Overcoming Abuse. This book contains the beginning of my testimony that started over a decade ago, in my early twenties. I was not raised in a Christian home and had never been to a Spirit-filled church as a child. I had been to church very few times, only when I went with another family. My mother never went to church not once in my childhood. I know it's difficult for many Christian believers to imagine that there are people out there that have absolutely no church background, but there are many of us out there.

Contrary to popular belief, not all of us are closed or cold to the Gospel of the Kingdom either. Many of us, your neighbors, co-workers and classmates have just never been introduced or given an appealing opportunity to come to know Jesus Christ. I thank God for the lady whose name I don't remember who obeyed God to witness to me over and over, no matter how many times I didn't respond. She would invite me to church and I would smile and thank her for the invite but never show up, but she just didn't give up. When I finally woke up and realized she was an answer to my prayers for escape from my troubled life, I ran her down to ask her where I could go to church. Her persistence paid off. While I may not know her name, God has me on her record book and all the people that I've lead to Christ. All the people I encourage each week to live lives of faith are also on her record in heaven! Praise God for her faithfulness to be a light!

I pray that as you read the detailed stories of my early life, that God will touch your heart and increase your faith in Him. I also hope that it will give you a fresh view of newcomers to the faith and a new passion to share this real Good News with those who are around you. You never know who you might be leading to Jesus....

SAMANTHA M. PHILLIPS

1 WHERE HE FOUND ME

My life had taken a downward spiral due to a series of bad decisions. In a nutshell, my childhood had been a crazy whirlwind of both positive experiences as well as some very negative ones. My father died when I was an infant, leaving my Japanese mother with no help to raise me in a country where she knew no one and had very little family. By the time I reached my teen years, the pressures of working day and night at menial manual labor jobs, extreme loneliness and her own troubled past caused my mother's behavior to change in a very negative way. Maybe it was the fear of me, the ONLY thing she felt she had left, growing up and leaving her like my sister did, that caused her to begin to try to suffocate me and my will for a life on my own, but it caused our relationship to be very strained.

With the anger and bitterness that had built up in me from my high school years being so full of trauma, emotional abuse and sometimes even physical abuse, as I turned 18, I was very happy to FINALLY be able to leave home and break free from her and the crazy environment my once happy childhood home had become.

I started off to what seemed like a pretty good start. I was so ambitious & my heart had been set on being two things since I was a little girl, a performer such as in acting, singing, modeling, etc and an attorney. I graduated high school in June and started college in July. I remember my friends were looking forward to taking off the summer and partying and me thinking, the quicker I start, the quicker I finish.

PROVERBS 17:21 Many are the plans in a person's heart, but it is the LORD's purpose that prevails.

Starting college in July, I made Dean's list my first semester and all seemed to be going well. However in my personal life, things were very bad. My mother kicked me out on my 18th birthday, literally on the actual day. I guess in her fear of being abandoned, she figured she would beat me to the punch. Not knowing where I would go, with all I owned in two black plastic garbage bags, I moved in with my high school boyfriend who was many years older than me. While I tried to concentrate on doing well in school, and working full time also to pay bills, I soon began to lose my grip on my well planned out life and things began to unravel quickly.

My boyfriend began to be very possessive soon after we moved in together. One day the possessive tendencies boiled over into him physically attacking me. I called the police and that was my last day there. I was so determined to not live in another abusive situation, after finally breaking free from the abuse of my childhood. Explaining my situation to the police who came, telling them I had no where to go, my mother had put me out, this guy put his hands on me and I refused to stay. Honestly, they tried to talk me into letting him "cool down" and then maybe coming back, but I let them know staying there was completely OUT of the question. Putting your hands on me was off limits and a complete deal breaker for me. I would NOT end up abused as I had been in my teen years, or so I thought.

They recommended a new youth shelter in our area. Their normal clientele was to be young adults and teens that were being released from Juvenile Detention Centers or whose behavioral issues were leaving their families with no choice but to put them out of their homes. I was their first client.

It was such a strange place to be in my life, the first of many strange places to be. It was a very large facility and the room where I was assigned had entire rows of bunk beds on both walls. Everything was brand new and I was the only one staying there. The counselors loved me and they were so excited to have their first client and me not be so rough for them. During this time, I continued to attend school, work and maintain my Dean's list GPA in legal studies.

After a short stay as the single resident and apple of the program's eye, one day the announcement came that another girl was being dropped off. This one was a parental surrender, which meant her mother was dropping her off. As she walked through the doors with her garbage bags with all her things in them just like I had, to my surprise and relief, I recognized her! We had known each other since the 4th grade! I lost touch with her once we went to different high schools, but what a relief to see a friendly face. Little did I know the traps of destruction for my life were being laid out in front of me.

My long lost childhood friend's familiarity with the hood was something I believed I really needed at that time. She was well connected to the drug game; her boyfriend of many years was one of the top traffickers in our entire region. The youth program was in one of the worst neighborhoods in Pittsburgh, where crime rates were sky high. I was harassed daily walking to and from the city bus stop to catch the bus to school, work and back to the shelter. Some days I would be followed by homeless men calling out and taunting me. Other days I would be bothered by just guys hanging out on the corners, cat calling but taking it too far to get up in my face, like nose to nose distance, saying things that scared me to the core. It was a miracle I didn't get raped or robbed. I stuck out like a sore thumb in the hood when I first arrived there.

I told her how bad things had been and she said she understood why. She told me I was a walking target in the hood going to and from the bus stop wearing business suits required for my college. She told me that I had better toughen up or else they were going to eat me alive. Basically, she began to teach me everything she knew. And just like everything else in my life, I love to learn and to learn quickly to acclimate to my environment. Boy, did I learn fast and well! Before I knew it, I had lost my identity.

Slowly, I began to identify with the street life I had only seen in movies as a young child. The music I listened to changed. This was in the years where "Gangsta" Rap was on the up rise and I was in the midst of a situation where the anger and power I felt when listening to it was exactly what I thought I needed to survive. It perpetuated what I felt in my heart with all the resentment and anger I had towards my mother. My love for Hip Hop had now led me to a place where my environment and circumstances combined with this anger filled, criminally-minded music began to change and undermine everything I had ever hoped to be in life.

I had spent so much of my life being mature beyond my years, focusing on having a great future since elementary school. Taking care of a mother whose mind was deteriorating and could not read or write English. I had been taking care of paying the bills, which meant adding things up and writing out money orders for the bills, since I was 10 years old. My mother didn't understand how to use a checking account, so we always used money orders to pay bills.

My plans for my great future always prevailed in the decisions I made. Don't get me wrong, I was a normal rebellious teenager so I did many things that were dumb but I always drew a line at where I believed I would be endangering my future plans. My desire for a better life and to be something great drove me to stay on track and get back on track quickly when I would slightly veer off.

But this time was different. I was by passing my normal boundaries and venturing out farther than was a safe distance from the shore. Before I knew it, I was carrying weapons, because in our hood, it was kill or be killed. To be completely honest, this life style intrigued me. It wasn't what the stereotypes tried to paint it as.

The young men I met who were running things, the tops of the drug dealing world in our region at the time, were highly intelligent and very driven for success also. They were business minded and believe it or not very disciplined. They would NEVER use drugs, because that would affect their bottom line and make them weak. They didn't smoke. They didn't drink often. These guys even ate healthy! They had to be wise with how they conducted business and who they allowed to know what they were doing. These weren't the dumb, slow-minded criminals portrayed in the ghetto flicks. These brothers were sharp. They were smart, they looked good and they had big things on their minds. To cover up the hundreds of thousands of dollars flowing through their hands, they would buy businesses, laundry mats all over the city, game arcades, car detail shops, car washes, anything that could launder money. They bought them and ran them well.

The ambition, the lure of the money, all of it was so exciting to me and I began to immerse myself in that culture. Soon that which I never thought I would do, I did. I dropped out of college. I wanted to spend more time with my new "family," that is what it felt like to me...a "family," something I never really had. I remember being sick to my stomach as I gave up on my dreams of graduating college and going on to law school but I ignored it and kept going.

It didn't take long, in less than a year; this world began to also crumble around me. I started seeing how dangerous things had really gotten, how as long as I was in good standing with them I was fine, but people who weren't would just flat out disappear. No bodies would ever be found, but their families would report them missing because they would just never be seen again. This highly intelligent group was also a very paranoid group. They suspected everyone all the time of selling them out and if they felt you were disloyal, that you may be a threat, you simply disappeared. To top it all off, I noticed that I had also picked up plain clothed detectives who followed me everywhere I went. I started being "detained" by local police officers for no reason. I would never tell them anything but just the fact that they kept picking me up and letting me go without any charges began to raise suspicion around me in my "family."

I knew I had to get out. I knew that if I didn't, I was either going to end up in jail or dead, so I reverted to my old "plan b." I always said that if I couldn't make it in college, I would join the Air Force like my father did. I called the recruiter and within another few months, at 19 years old, I left for basic training. This was well over a year out of high school and a LONG way away from how I left high school with so much focus and hope for the future. Now, just over a year later, I was running from the mess I had made of my life.

I remember the smell of the pre-dawn morning air in San Antonio, Texas that first morning of basic training. I hadn't slept at all the night before half out of excitement and half out of fear. I was exhausted and then the yelling began. The drill instructors yelled and yelled again. I was in a very strange place in this walk of my young life. All our freedom is taken away in basic training, in their effort to instill in us the privilege and price of freedom, what we that serve or have served in the Armed Forces fight to maintain in our country. While it was not easy, once again, I had found a family and this one wasn't illegal which is always a good thing.

While I had left Pittsburgh far behind me, and I was now in a new environment and family, the hurts of my past, the messed up mentality I had adopted, it all followed me to the Air Force. I began to conform to the young airmen's technical school lifestyle, which was to study hard, work hard but to play even harder when off duty. I began to drink and smoke heavily and enjoyed the low ratio of women to men. They said back then that there was only one woman to every eight men in the Air Force and out of that 1 in every 8, there weren't many "pretty" girls. So if you were cute, you were like a queen on a throne. Combine that with no boundaries, no morals and a hurt heart and you have a recipe for destruction.

I was literally looking for love in all the wrong places. I had hardened my heart so far from who I used to be. I used to be a faithful romantic who believed in love. I had the same boyfriend from 8th grade until my freshman year of college. Now I had hardened my heart and played the role of one who believed sex and love did not have to go together. Only weak women expected a guy to be their boyfriend because they had sex or showed interest. Strong women knew better. I decided that "love" was a game and it looked like the only ones who won were usually the players. So I decided that if there was a game to be played, I was going to play it, and I was going to win. My convictions to not be the type of girl who slept around kept me from getting as bad as some with multiple sex partners but playing with men's hearts was fun, or so I thought.

The problem with this whole scenario is, that while I played the role, in my heart of hearts, I knew it was all wrong. I was in denial, but I knew it was wrong. Guys would date me and buy me gifts and meanwhile they'd have other girls on the side that I would find out about. So I decided I can do the same thing. When the guy who assumed he was my boyfriend would find out I was dating more than him and try to get upset, I'd let him know all I knew he was doing on the side and would say something to the effect of "I didn't trip on you or even ask you a question about it when I found out, I just figured we were cool like that so I'm just doing what you're doing."

For the most part, it felt great to not be the weak one, to see the looks of surprise on their cheating, double-standard having faces, but in my heart, I secretly longed for someone to love me, to love me enough to NOT have girls on the side, to love me enough to say he wanted to be with only me and not play games of assumption so he could do his thing.

So I played my games and I thought I was in control. There were one or two legitimate guys along the way, but I was too blind to see them because I was too busy playing them before they could play me. I thought I was in control. But these ungodly lifestyles have a way of lying to you. In reality I was setting myself up for major downfall. Soon my time in technical school was ending and I was receiving orders to transfer to a new base in Virginia. I remember taking a week off before leaving Texas to just be alone to rethink the fast lane I had been traveling in, to consider what I should do going forward. By the end of that week, I had decided I needed to slow it way down, leave the game playing in Texas and get serious about my life. Little did I know, my life was about to take an abrupt halt that would change everything and show me that I was NOT in control.

When I arrived at my next duty station, I quickly met someone else who was very different. He was my type when it came to good looks and he was very interested in me. I went full steam ahead with this new guy, who was saying all the things I had always wanted to hear: *"I don't want anyone but you! You are the only one I want to be with, I want to marry you!"* I had many proposals before but never from anyone I took seriously. It still makes me wonder why I believed this one, maybe because I had decided to quit running. Unfortunately, that is the thing about making bad decisions, you don't get better; you get worse.

Less than two months into our marriage was the first time I caught my new husband cheating. I was devastated because I was pregnant already and all the sudden the reality that I had made a mistake marrying someone I didn't know came flooding into my mind. The words, "you reap what you sow" kept playing in the back of my mind thinking of how badly I had treated people in my past. Guilt caused me to question whether I deserved what I was getting. He was such a smooth talker! I believed everything he said, every excuse he made, and every lie he told.

He would strategically let me know the horrible things that happened to him in his childhood, telling me it made it hard for him to function as a husband. That he was working on it, that he loved me and that he needed me to help him make it through. I fell for it hook, line and sinker. He needed me and I was going to be there for him. At the same time, he also began to criticize me, my looks, and my faithfulness. It was always when he was angry and then would apologize with all the stories of his past and how he needed me to help him be better. Meanwhile the cheating continued and what I didn't know was a cycle of abuse was beginning that would almost take my life.

You don't know your self-esteem is being eroded until one day you wake up and realize you are putting up with stuff you would normally never put up with but also lack the confidence or strength to walk away. I was the type of girl who didn't put up with any mess! I was the type of girl who didn't love easy because I was strong. I had worked so hard to not end up abused. How could this be happening to ME?

After my son was born, the cheating and the bad treatment continued but yet I wanted to believe it would get better. There was girl after girl and the harsh words had turned into me being grabbed and slammed on a wall or pushed down and eventually turned into me being slapped and hit. I realized that I was in very deep trouble. I had started devising a plan to leave him, to try to escape.

Just as I was beginning to see a light at the end of the tunnel, my own plan again collapsed when I found out I was pregnant again, despite being on birth control. I was devastated. This is when depression hit my life horribly. I had begun to lose my will to live. The cheating continued and his horrible treatment escalated. We fought constantly over the cheating and the fights were almost always physical.

What people don't realize who have never been the victim of spousal abuse is the prison of the cycle of it. They abuse you. You swear you are leaving. They demean you when you say it, and then they begin to apologize and beg you back. They tell you how much they love you, how sorry they are and go overboard to show you how much they love you. Flowers, showing up at the job to take you to lunch, all those things a man in "love" does. When you are caught in the cycle of abuse, you live for those good parts of the cycle. You continue to believe for the day that your abuser will stay in that "good" part. The day when he will mean what he said when he apologized and finally be better because we, the women who love them, did what good women do and loved them back to life.

The problem is that without divine intervention and the man's willingness to follow that divine intervention, those cycles rarely end well or change. The episodes of violence escalate as he becomes more confident that you will not leave and the apologies and romance decrease. During my second pregnancy, I often prayed for death. I was so distraught, I just wanted to go to sleep and never wake up.

During that time, literally only on the days that I would pray and cry out to God saying, "if you are real, then please don't make me suffer anymore! Please just let me die!" The next day this lady I only met once or twice would show up and invite me to church and try to talk to me about Jesus. I didn't want to hear it but she was nice and I didn't want to be rude. Oftentimes when I saw her, I would still be distressed from the night's episodes the day previous and I would literally avoid her when I saw her coming, if I could get away with it, I would hide from her. I didn't realize that God was answering my prayers, not with death but with an opportunity for new life!

Finally one day, at the point of utter distress, as I cried out in prayer to God sitting in my car at 1AM in the base chapel parking lot again, pleading with swollen eyes and face, "please God don't let me continue to suffer! Please God please just let me die" as I fell asleep in my car where I had ran to escape the abuse of the night. When I woke up, I can't say that I heard a voice, but I remember it dawning on me that this lady was my answer to prayer! I suddenly realized that I needed to get to church right away. Sure enough, like always, as I walked down the hall at my job the day after I cried out to God in prayer, I saw her! Except this time, instead of running to hide, I ran to her and told her I wanted to come to church and to please give me the address, which she gladly did.

I started going to church most Sundays after that, I loved the feeling of peace and love I felt there. I asked my ex to come and he did on a few occasions. I remember when the altar calls to salvation would come, he would whisper in my ear *"don't you raise your hand and make a fool out of yourself! You don't know anything about this Bible and I do, trust me, you are going to make a fool out of yourself. KEEP THAT HAND DOWN – I MEAN IT!"* So reluctantly, although I really did want to give my heart to the Lord, I wouldn't raise my hand. I had such an assurance that this was the place we would find the help we needed but he was refusing to allow us to get connected or at least he was trying to prevent it.

Then one Sunday, he refused to go to church, but said I could go which was different from what he usually would allow. Normally if he didn't feel like going, I wasn't allowed to go either. Thinking back, he probably had a new girlfriend he wanted to talk to and wanted me out of the house, but God had something in store for me!

That Sunday, in January of 1997, 7 months pregnant with my second child, I was finally free to lift my hand for the altar call and my life changed forever! In fact I literally RAN to the altar for prayer to receive Jesus Christ as Lord and Savior that day. I remember the pastor playfully saying *"Well praise the Lord, I don't believe I've ever seen a pregnant woman move that fast!"* But he had no idea what I was running from and how glad I was to be running to Jesus! The love I so desperately longed for all of my life now flooded my soul! FINALLY THIS IS WHAT REAL LOVE FEELS LIKE!

Jesus picked me up at the point of literal utter distress. A young girl who had wronged so many people in her day and needed forgiveness, who had an entire childhood of pain, hurt and anger caged up inside and needed healing and deliverance. I was a girl who was trapped in abuse, and had one young child with another on the way and needed hope for the future. This was the girl who ran to the altar that day. I was a girl who grew up in the trailer park and ended up in the hood. I was a girl who had been involved closely with people who were violent criminals. I had done so many things I wasn't proud of. What would God want with me? After all, this is all my own doing! I made my choices, I made my proverbial bed and now I was lying in it, actually dying in it. I didn't deserve new life; I was too emotionally and mentally weak to make a new one for myself! I was of no use! What would Jesus want with me? However by His unlimited and unexplainable loving grace and mercy, He wanted ALL of me! He loved me despite all I had done. He loved me despite how messed up I had caused my life to be! He forgave, He healed me and He gave me hope! "*Amazing Grace how sweet the sound, that saved a wretch like me*" was no longer just a famous song, it became life and love to me that day in Northern California. All things became new that day! My circumstances didn't change overnight but the journey of new

life had begun!

2 HOW HE TOUCHED ME

There was so much wrong with me from a Christian perspective. When I got saved, I was totally un-churched. I was not raised in a Christian home, I had not been exposed to the Christian lifestyle and had absolutely no idea what a Christian Worldview was. All these years later, I now serve God as a leader in His Kingdom and having observed how some churches teach and treat new converts, I realize how the Lord protected me and caused me to have a very unique experience in being taught how to live.

When I got saved, I was a hip-hop club girl. While my life was in turmoil, I also went to the clubs every weekend with very little exception. It was my escape. I would dance the night away to secular hip-hop and rap every Friday and Saturday and then be in church on Sunday morning. The world I lived in and the songs and movies of my culture formed my definition of life, beauty and behavior.

This world was very different from the Christian world. I was saved, I loved Jesus with all my heart, but I hadn't yet been exposed to Godly culture or lifestyle. In my world, short skirts and bare midriffs were acceptable and popular. In my world, cursing in conversation was not only accepted, it was almost an art form. Being flirtatious, social drinking and violent and sexually charged music was desirable. The transition into living a Godly lifestyle doesn't happen overnight, especially when dealing with someone who is un-churched and has no idea what the Godly standards even are.

When Jesus touched my life, He didn't do it with criticism or with hitting me with a rulebook like many religious people do to new believers. He did it with His love. With my troubled life, not having ever felt unconditional love, Jesus Christ flooded my heart with the real power of His love. There was no doubt that I wanted out of my abusive relationship, but I felt trapped. It was like there were invisible bands that would allow me to get so far, but then would prevent me from breaking free sending me catapulting back to where I came from.

There were nights I would swear I was leaving my abuser for good. Those nights I would fall asleep in my car crying out to God. They started with me packing my things, grabbing my sleeping baby son and saying I was leaving. I remember driving and as soon I as I would get only a few miles from home, the voices of fear and doubt would begin to speak to me and having no real plan of escape nor confidence I could make it on my own; I would turn the car around in defeat and return to the abuse. I was returning to be mocked and to fall into depression and disgust with myself for being so weak and going back.

However, when Jesus saved me, His love began to change and strengthen me in a way that human words cannot properly capture. My life was still going through all the same turmoil, but now it affected me in a different way. It used to rock me to my core because I had no core! I didn't know who I really was. I had no one to rely on or lean to for guidance, love or help. Jesus Christ became my core. He touched me with his real love and real identity. When I acknowledged who He was, He showed me who I was. Now, though my situations were not yet better and in fact, slightly worse, I finally had hope for a new life! The sense of His love that flooded my heart and expelled my sorrow is one that is almost indescribable, but that is exactly what I experienced. Then this hunger, this yearning to learn from His Word began to grow.

I was so hungry to know more about Him, His Word, His desire for my life! What is really most amazing to me is, at the risk of offending some judgmental, legalistic "church" people, His initial outpouring in my life was not one of rules of what I should and shouldn't do. There was no focus on my dress code or the music I listened to. Some say maybe I wasn't listening to Him, maybe I was determined to stay carnal, but neither of those things were true. I was sincerely hungry and I was sincerely hearing from Him. The things I needed to change weren't due to rebellion; I didn't know what the standards were to rebel against them. However, I was having regular encounters with Him. He was speaking to me and teaching me in His Word powerfully.

The lessons He imparted dealt with the depth of His love, the vastness of His Power, the fullness of His care & reliability of His provision and not with the externals of my life. He first did an inside work and then an outside work! Empty religion focuses on the outside, too often ignoring the inside.

Matthew 23:26 Blind Pharisee! First clean the inside of the cup and dish, and then the outside also will be clean.

Eventually the externals of my life changed, but for many months, my initial teaching and impartation from His Spirit and Word were not regarding the external stuff. I was a young woman trapped in an abusive relationship with two babies to raise. I didn't need empty religion; I needed the power of real relationship!

I remember the day His Word began to leap off the pages and become life to me. Reading Matthew the sixth chapter, I learned that I didn't need to fear where my provision would come from. He taught me that if He cared for the lilies in the field and the birds in the air, then He would also care for me, His child. That was LIFE CHANGING revelation for me! I sat there in tears as I read it. This was God's Word, His written promise to me telling me He would take care of me! I finally had what I needed to be FREE!!! The promise of provision, not from a man but from God Himself!

People who have never been in an abusive situation often misunderstand women who are trapped in abusive relationships. Before I ended up there, I also was someone who was very judgmental of those who were victims of abuse. I, like many others thought that only "weak" women stayed in these situations. After all, if someone mistreats you, why not just leave? That is what I did back when I was 18 and a freshman in college.

The reality is, when you are really caught up in abuse, it's simply not that easy.

Unfortunately, people don't understand the subtle day-by-day, moment-by-moment, wearing down of the self-esteem that happens. They don't understand the guilt trip that is placed on the abused or the feeling of hopelessness that you won't be able to make it without your abuser. On the days the guilt works, you fluctuate from feeling like you did something to deserve your abuser being angry to feeling like if you leave him, he will be lost and it's your responsibility to love him back to life.

When guilt doesn't work, then fear steps up and kills your will for better. Fear begins to speak and say that you won't be able to make it without the support of your abuser. If that angle doesn't work, fear says that he may find you and kill you or hurt your children or family. Low self-esteem, fear and guilt work like a tri-fold yoke of bondage to keep the abused trapped.

This is where the love of God came in and set me free! He began to love me and speak to my heart and let me know how valuable I was to Him. He replaced what used to be self esteem with something more solid: "God" (in me) esteem! He revealed my Father to me and therefore my identity! I was a daughter of the Most High! I had a very rich and very powerful Daddy and He loved me so much! He didn't want me to be abused and promised to take care of me!

One of the things my abuser used to keep me feeling bad about myself, was my past. "You're nothing but a ghetto gangster girl!" or "You have

TWO kids now! NOBODY is ever going to want you!" He was always throwing the things I was ashamed of from my past in my face as a way to tell me I had no right to expect more or want any better than this abusive life he was offering me. But again, the love of God undermined all of his efforts!

Because of Jesus Christ, I learned I was FORGIVEN!!! He may not have understood or recognized it – but what he thought didn't matter because GOD HIMSELF told me in His Word that I was forgiven! No longer was I a slave to my past! No longer did my mistakes and shortcomings disqualify me from freedom! There was REAL POWER in the Blood of Jesus to wash away my past!

SAMANTHA M. PHILLIPS

3 HOW HE CHANGED ME

The love of God changed me so much that it gave me the strength to step out and break free from my abusive relationship, trusting in Him to be my provider.   He had built me up where everyone else had always torn me down.   He showed me love when everyone else showed criticism.   His love changed me from the inside out!

I had tried so many things to change my own life. I had fought with all I had in me to make sure that my life would never end up in abuse. What I found out after all my wasted efforts was, it is absolutely impossible to have the circumstances of your life change without your heart being changed. The reality is that because I had not forgiven my mother for the abuse of my teen years, I was perpetuating what I hated in my own life. I was filled with resentment, unforgiveness, anger and offense. So no matter how badly I wanted my life to be better, all I could really manage to do was to come up with temporary changes for long-term issues. It was like expecting apples from a lemon tree. I could run around taking all the lemons off with all my might, but when the conditions of the season were right, lemons is what was going to come from the tree. Unless you change the root, you will never change the fruit.

What the presence of the love of God first did in my life, was change me, by causing me to forgive and make a choice to love those who had once hurt me so deeply. I had to forgive my mother, regardless of all the things she had done. I had to forgive my ex, regardless of the depth of the pain and betrayal he had inflicted in my life. The single most powerful act towards breaking the cycles of abuse was to forgive.

For some it feels and seems very much impossible to forgive those who have done us wrong on such a deep level. After all, these are the people who violated our trust of them. These are the people who were supposed to love and nurture us or love and protect us and they did the exact opposite! I remember how it felt to feel that I could never forgive my mother. Before I understood the love of God and the depth of His forgiveness towards me, to forgive was to let my abusers off the hook. They didn't deserve forgiveness after all they had done!

But the love of God changed my heart. He changed me with His forgiveness towards me despite all I had done. He loved me when I didn't know what love was and certainly didn't love myself. Through his Word, I realized that to forgive them was not to let them off the hook, but it was to let myself off the hook. By not forgiving them, my life was doomed to continue to repeat the cycles of disappointment and hurt. His forgiveness flowed to me and then through me to those who had hurt me the most. This was one of the first MAJOR steps taken towards a real life change.

There was so much that needed to change about me. As I already mentioned, my entire identity had become so confused. I had no idea who I was created to be and how that person acted. The Lord didn't change me by the judgmental glances and occasional rebukes from my sisters and brothers in the church. In fact those things really worked against a life change. I really thank God that I never judged the realness of God by the fakeness of His people! I understood that people have issues, no matter where or who they are. I was accustomed to "haters" and "jealous fellas" in the world and I honestly wasn't at all surprised to find them in the church.

Church people who are judgmental and critical often hide under the reasoning that they are trying to help those they criticize. They don't want you to go to hell or to get into trouble so they scoff at your clothing, your music choices, your friends, etc. The problem is, there is no place in Scripture where Jesus handled new believers like this. In fact, He sharply rebuked the religious people of his day for focusing on the outside of the cup while not dealing with the inside.

In fact, the only people Jesus did openly rebuke were these same religious people who were so quick to judge and criticize the weak. Because I did understand that the people in the church were not who I was there for, but for the God of the church, I didn't allow the criticism and persecution to push me out. While it was not

God's will for me to be criticized and treated harshly by those who claimed to be His, it WAS God's will for me to change!

There is a delicate balance between what people claim is the "grace" of God and the opposite of legalism. Legalism always kills the power of the Word in the believers' lives. However an ungodly blanket for sin wrongly called "grace" is also equally as damaging. God DOES desire for us to change but He doesn't want us to change simply because we don't want men to judge us. God wants us to allow His Word, the revelation of who He is and who He has called us to be, to CHANGE us from the inside out.

I was so steeped in hip-hop culture when I first was born again. I was very young, just 22 years old. I loved hip-hop music, the image and the culture. There were a handful of people who took it upon themselves to try to change me, but they always came with judgmentalism about what I shouldn't be doing or wearing. When I asked them to show it to me in the Bible, they never had any answers or references.

It caused me to throw out what they were saying, even though I now realize that they were correct about some of what I shouldn't do. Because they had no real revelation of their own, they couldn't share any substance with me. All they could offer was the regulations they had learned from other church people. The problem with that is, regulations multiply empty religion and fall short of real change.

Revelation is what solidifies right relationship with God and produces real change in the life of the believer.   Regulations are man given. Revelation is God given. Revelation is the "ah ha!" moment when the Word of God all the sudden makes sense for your life and you realize and receive instruction on how to live. Religion is man's way of trying to reach God and is void of revelation. Relationship is God's way of reaching man and is the only thing that can produce revelation. Revelation equals real change!

I was so hungry to know more about the Lord. That hunger produced a deep heart-felt desire to change. I wanted to learn what it meant to live how He wanted me to live. Once I learned the term "holy" I wanted to know from Him what it meant to live a holy lifestyle. It was a process and not an overnight event. But as I studied His Word and spoke to Him regularly, He began to teach me and give me revelation about life.

Self-destructive behaviors stopped because I received the revelation that I was His daughter and I was bought with a price. My body was not my own, it belonged to God and it was His delicate temple. I was God's Property! I didn't stop smoking, drinking, and all the rest because someone said it was a sin to do so. I stopped for two reasons: #1 I realized my worth #2 His love satisfied the longing of my soul so that I had no need for destructive, carnal fulfillment. Now with Him as my Lord, to lower myself to receive fulfillment in any other way than from His presence seemed so gross and dirty. In the beginning when I did slip and do things I had already repented for, the horrible feeling of exchanging the real for the counterfeit made me stop slipping. I enjoyed His presence so much that anything less was mediocre.

As the LORD removed my need for the destructive behaviors of the flesh, He also began to build me in His principles for living, His wisdom. He began to teach me "how to act" as we used to say in my old neighborhoods. As I began to study His Word, looking for the revelation for how to live, His principles began to mold and shape me into His image. Soon, I didn't see the world the same. I didn't see ANYTHING the same. I thought before I spoke. I felt compassion for people who used to make me furious. I wanted to serve others and also be the best at everything I did to honor and glorify God through my life. I saw love, family, money, health, and entertainment, literally

EVERYTHING differently. Suddenly what used to be appealing became appalling and anything less than God's best was simply not good enough.

The Word of God through revelation brought out the absolute best in me and is still polishing, shaping and molding me every day that I stay hungry for His revelation for life. Some of the persecution I have faced in recent years has been from family members or old acquaintances who remember me for the horrible person I used to be. They see me now and don't believe what they see because it is SO extremely different. They just don't understand that when a person gets real revelation, the changes that happen defy natural possibilities and generational tendencies. The Word of God alone did NOT change me. Right revelation of the Word of God for my life is what

changed me and it will change your life too!

4 HOW HE EMPOWERED ME

Sometimes people improperly limit God's power to emotional displays at church. I understand that these emotional displays are a result of our souls being touched with the Word and us wanting to show how thankful we are for the Word. While some argue that this form of Christianity is not fruitful, I must say that I disagree. Being able to leap for joy at the thought of God's

Word to impact and change what was "supposed to happen" has tremendous benefits to the soul of the believers. It gets your mind off the problems or situations and causes you to shout and have a great time. This shift from negative thinking to positive thinking and celebration is very fruitful and not to be diminished.

At the same time, emotional outbursts alone cannot empower you beyond the length of the emotional high. As soon as the euphoria wears off, you are left thinking the same and therefore reacting the same, doomed to repeat the same fruitless cycles of being down cast and then getting to church to "get your praise on!" God did not send His Word for you to get emotionally charged but remain the same.

The revelation of His Word that He used to change me is the same thing He used to empower me. This is what is amazing about living a life for God and makes it more addictive than any drug in the world. When you have right revelation of His Word and you are committed to serving His purpose, He releases very real, tangible power in your life.

This is the power to overcome every negative situation in your life! This is the power of His protection guarding you against even the plot of your enemies to harm you! This is the power that gives you the ability to accomplish what you never thought you could! There is a song saying there is power in the Blood of the Lamb, but it would be more accurate to say there is power in the REVELATION of the Blood of the Lamb!

God empowered me through the same revelation He changed me with. In the early stages of being born again, there were things that were a struggle for me to stop doing at first. However once I got a right revelation of His Word concerning it, I also received the power, the strength to walk in agreement with it. Right revelation also empowered me to break the strongholds of abuse in my life and gave me the courage to run towards new life.

When I read Matthew 6 for the first time after having my eyes opened to His revelation, those words leapt off the page, into my heart and gave me power! Through so much abuse, pain and humiliation I stayed in a horrible situation because I felt I lacked the power, the strength to break free. I feared not only for my personal well-being but for the well-being of my two very young children. If I had been alone, it would have been easy to take a chance at freedom when it was just my life at stake, but as a mother, what caused me to fear the most was the thought of not being able to provide for my children or to threaten their safety. I believe any mother who loves their children can relate. If the enemy can't paralyze you with fear for your own life, he will try to stop you with fear for your children. However when the REVELATION of Matthew 6:25-34 hit me, I received literal power to not be afraid and to trust God with not only my life, but also the life of my children.

Matthew 6:25 "Therefore I tell you, do not worry about your life, what you will eat or drink; or about your body, what you will wear. Is not life more than food, and the body more than clothes? 26 Look at the birds of the air; they do not sow or reap or store away in barns, and yet your heavenly Father feeds

them. Are you not much more valuable than they? 27 Can any one of you by worrying add a single hour to your life? 28 "And why do you worry about clothes? See how the flowers of the field grow. They do not labor or spin. 29 Yet I tell you that not even Solomon in all his splendor was dressed like one of these. 30 If that is how God clothes the grass of the field, which is here today and tomorrow is thrown into the fire, will he not much more clothe you—you of little faith? 31 So do not worry, saying, 'What shall we eat?' or 'What shall we drink?' or 'What shall we wear?' 32 For the pagans run after all these things, and your heavenly Father knows that you need them. 33 But seek first his kingdom and his righteousness, and all these things will be given to you as well. 34 Therefore do not worry about tomorrow, for tomorrow will worry about itself. Each day has enough trouble of its own.

The revelation of this Word released power! Not only power to believe and step out on what I believed, but power that released miraculous provision for us as well. The Revelation of His provision and promise hit me so great, I left my abusive situation with nothing but $200 to my name, my 2 year old, my 3 month old and all I could fit into my small Toyota Tercel.

I wish I could tell you that immediate blessing dropped out of the sky the day I left, in fact it did not. However the power released through the revelation caused me to press on and see the hand of God in my life! Anytime you make a decision to walk in revelation, there is often what seems to be a flood of natural circumstances and situations that come to try to get you to shrink back from your revelation. However when you allow the revelation to empower you, shrinking back is not an option!

Hebrews 10: 39 But we do not belong to those who shrink back and are destroyed, but to those who have faith and are saved.

I fled my abusive situation on revelation, drove across 3 states and wound up in Central Florida. I thought I could rely on family to help me and found that to not be a safe or reliable place. After only weeks of stepping out on the right revelation of God's Word in Matthew 6, I found myself checking into a local women & children's homeless shelter.

That first night there, I waited until my children fell asleep so as to not frighten them and I began to weep. I cried and spoke to the Lord and said, "Lord, I've trusted you, I stepped out on your word! How did I end up here? Now I have nothing!" He spoke to me so clearly and said "Everything you had before, you got on your own, or man gave it to you. I had to allow it all to fall away because it didn't come from me. From this day forward, everything you receive will be from me and no man will ever be able to take it from you" The power of my original right revelation produced more revelation that released more power to endure and overcome! From that day forward, despite the humiliating position of living in a homeless shelter, I held my head high and experienced the joy of the Lord daily as I went forward every day, looking for His provision, looking for where He would open the door for me and yes the power of right revelation produced! Doors opened and my life has never been the same! I will share the details of those events in the next chapter.

So much power was released to cause things to work in my favor as a result of operating in right revelation of who He is and His character.   The

Lord's greatest desire is to be acknowledged for the fullness of His character in each individual's life. Within weeks in a time when unemployment was very high, I had a decent job. Within another couple weeks, I was offered a full scholarship that included everything: tuition, books and even subsidized rent on an apartment. This scholarship program was only for former military service men and women and was a very selective program. I applied and of course, the power of right revelation was in operation and I received the scholarship. It was in this program that I eventually met my wonderful "Boaz" husband and father of our six children, Michael. He loved GOD, me and my children as his own, eventually adopting my oldest two as his own. We began our relationship serving God together and as soon as we got married, it was like a fast track to full time ministry was ignited. Over 12 years later at the time I am writing this book, we have seen the greatness of the power of God released by right revelation of His Word, literally catapult us from a very meager existence to a powerful, wealthy and purpose filled place! I am going to recap the stories in detail of "How He Blessed Me" in the next chapter.

God empowered me to get back up after being cast down so many times. He empowered me to overcome the horrible cycles of abuse in my life and the lives of my children. He empowered me to walk in His purpose and experience the fullness of real abundant life through the power released because of right revelation!

What's wonderful is, God doesn't limit His Word from producing for people based on any externals or judgments of men. The sole thing that will empower God's word in your life is your own revelation of it. If you lack revelation, you will always lack power. Knowing what the Word says is not enough. You must know He is talking directly to you and take it for what it is all the way to the core of your being. When the Word permeates beyond your church experience and begins to apply to how you see life, it becomes revelation in your life and therefore releases power for real change!

John 6:63 The Spirit gives life; the flesh counts for nothing. The words I have spoken to you—they are full of the Spirit and life.

5 HOW HE BLESSED ME

Through all the Lord has done in forgiving me, as messed up as I was, setting me free from the cycles of abuse and sin & protecting me against the threats of my past, the thing that has overwhelmed me the most is how much He desired and still does for my life to be blessed. Its always perplexed me how much He loves me despite of me and how much because He loves me, He wants me to have and be the absolute best for Him.

The very first scripture He touched my heart with revelation on was Matthew 6 as I've mentioned often in the book. I realized that I had NOTHING to worry about concerning earthly needs, that GOD Himself promised in His Word that if I would trust Him and not worry, that He would provide for me. I guess I never realized how uncommon it is for a person to REALLY believe this to the core, to have a REAL revelation of this until I became a pastor many years later. However when I read this, it was so simple to me. God is the One who created all things and is in control of all things, and HE made me a promise in His Word, a DOCUMENTED promise, that He would provide. I believed it and I've received it, in abundance.

When I stepped out in faith to leave my abusive situation with my two infant sons, I only had $200 and the things I could fit in a small Toyota Tercel. I had to leave everything behind in order to get out right away. God had put an urgency in my heart to move quickly and those promptings very well may have saved my life and the lives of my first two sons. I headed to Florida because I had a relative, who I didn't know well, we hadn't grown up together, but who was in my eyes my only option.

When I arrived in Florida, at first things seemed okay, but taking on a single mom who was still clearly rough around the edges and two young children is a lot for someone who you are in close relationship with, let alone someone you are not. Soon that environment also began to become very unhealthy, especially for my children, so once again, I had to operate by faith and leave.

I had been searching for work daily, with no baby sitter, taking my two year old & 3-month-old son with me everywhere I went. Needless to say, most employers weren't impressed with a young single mother who didn't have any family support and no baby sitters. I also looked into public assistance, and in visiting one of the agencies, had received a list of places that provide all types of assistance, including shelters. It was late one night after an unfortunate episode in the house I was staying in, that I found myself calling the numbers on that list, crying and needing to find a safe place for my children and me.

I called place after place, telling my story and expressing my need for help. Place after place told me they had no rooms available and couldn't help me. I was becoming distressed, and wondering if I may have to sleep in my car with my children. And I just kept praying in between each phone call and asking God to help me. As the tears rolled down my face, I finally got an answer at one place. What I did NOT know was that this was one of the best and nicest programs or shelters for women and children in the area. The conditions were the best and they were very much Christ centered. They had a three-year waiting list of people wanting to get in. Of course, when I called this place was also full, but the lady who answered the phone was different than those I had spoken to at other places. She really listened to my story. She compassionately asked me questions to find out more about my situation.

And then after a long pause, she said, "Okay, listen to me, I don't want you to sleep in your car with your children, come here tonight, I am NOT supposed to do this, but come here and we can put you in the nursery area, but you will have to sleep on the floor. There are cribs for your children, but you will have to sleep on the floor. We cannot house you the next day though, I will have to see if I can find somewhere else for you to go, but you cannot stay here longer than just tonight."

As the sense of relief flooded me, FINALLY someone who would help me, I thanked her, got in my car and started driving to their facility. As I drove I cried much and all I knew to do was to thank God out loud as I cried. I had no idea what the next day was going to bring. As I drove I would glance at my two babies in their car seats, once again with all I owned in my car! What in the WORLD am I doing? Was I crazy to think I could be free? What will I do tomorrow, she said I couldn't stay?! Then His voice quietly reminded me from my one revelation I had of Matthew 6 not to worry about tomorrow. So I dried my eyes and drove on.

The floor was so hard and cold in that nursery room. It was covered by just a thin layer of industrial carpeting and felt like there was no padding at all. I settled the boys in the cribs in the room, and once they fell asleep, I took the blanket and pillow the lady gave me and laid on that cold, hard floor. Once again, the tears began to flow as I laid there on the floor. I quietly cried out to God, "I'm on the FLOOR in a homeless shelter God! I fought so hard all my life not to be in this type of position and now I am here with my two children! I trusted you GOD!!! How did I end up here!?"

His loving answer burned into my heart and those Words have carried me to this day. He said to me "Everything you've had before now was through the hands of men. I had to allow it to all go away, but from this day forward, everything you receive will be from Me and no man will ever be able to take it away. This is NOT your end, it's your new beginning." WOW! Not my end, but my new beginning. In an instant, those Words from His heart to mine, drove the desperation and disappointment out immediately. I dried my tears like a little girl who's Daddy just gave her an ice cream cone after she fell and scraped her knee. His Words were real to me and they were comfort.

My view of my situation changed instantly because I heard my Daddy's voice.

The next day, when I woke up, I folded my borrowed blanket and put it with my borrowed pillow, gathered my babies and headed to the lobby of the shelter. When I approached the front desk, I was asked to sit and wait in the lobby until someone could talk to me. The lady from the night before came and let me know she was working on some things and would let me know if she could find something for me but asked me not to leave.

This particular shelter for women and children was very nice and the women who stayed there seemed to really enjoy it. Women passed me by me as I sat in the lobby and observing them I saw women who looked like they had been through very hard times just like I had. But they had found a place of refuge in this wonderful program. It was in the lobby that day that I found out that they had a waiting list three years long to get in. It was in the lobby that day that I learned that the other places of the same type were not as nice and were also not safe. As the people I spoke with let me know how unsafe the other places were, I began to wonder if I really wanted to find a "spot" at any of them. Of course, I began to pray as I waited and then the news came.

In this program that has a three-year waiting list, where women didn't want to leave and fought to get in, one of the residents had not come back the night before. The lady who let me in explained that even though this was the case, she would have to get special approval for me to be allowed to take her place because there were others on the list that had been there before me. I would have to wait and see what was decided. Again, I began to pray and God gave me peace. Then the news came, the first of a lifetime of provision and blessing miracles I would experience, the decision had been made to make an exception for me. I was given a room at the refuge of the Christian Rescue Mission!

After just a few weeks in the program, I had already began to defy the odds. Most of the women in the program stay there for at least a year. Because of the comfort level of the accommodations there, many people don't seem to want to leave. I met women who had lived there for two and three years! While I greatly appreciated the refuge they provided, I also knew in my heart that God had better for me. I continued my diligent job search and finally landed a job working evenings for an airline based in Orlando.

I finally started seeing that indeed me and my children would be okay. While I trusted God with all my heart, I had no idea to expect anything more than His love and covering. I didn't realize how blessed His covering really is! My plan was to save up enough money to get a small apartment for my children and me and basically get "back on my feet" and start over again on a normal life. I didn't realize God had MUCH more in His plan for me.

It was during this time that I was enjoying God's presence in my life so very much. While my situation seemed so bad, even losing the car I had, having no money to make the payments, His love was literally melting my heart and taking so many layers of hurt and lies out of my mind. I went to church every Sunday hungry for Him and I came back full every Sunday. I read His Word day and night and literally carried my Bible with me almost everywhere I went so that I could read it every spare moment. There was one day, as I was riding home in the Rescue Mission van that I was talking with the Lord, passing by a corner in one of the worst neighborhood's in the city and I was overwhelmed with thanksgiving for His presence in my life. I began to speak to him in my heart and let Him know how much I desperately needed His presence with me, I literally said to Him in reflection of all I had once held on to and what I no longer had, "Lord I'd rather live in a cardboard box on the corner with you than to live life without you!"

Nothing was worth losing His Presence in my life! I was content with just His presence, little did I know how much being in His presence would bring into my life!

One night after work, I was picking up my children from the night daycare facility when the second great miracle of provision I saw in my life happened. Because I got off work so late at night, the Rescue Mission van would pick me up from a near-by bus stop, take me to my daycare to pick up my children and then back to the Rescue Mission. As the van with the big words "RESCUE MISSION" painted on the sides waited outside, I would go in every night, pick up my sleeping babies, carry them one by one to the van and go back to the Mission, but this night was different. As I went inside, a young couple, a little older than me was also there picking up their baby. I had never seen them before and knew that their baby was not a regular for night care. As I began to pack up my youngest son, the wife of the couple randomly said to me *"You're not from here are you?"* It was a little odd, being that I didn't know them, but there was something very kind about her and her husband, something different about them. *"No, I'm not."* I answered. *"You're ex-military aren't you?"* Ok, now she was freaking me out a little bit! *"Yes....umm how did you know that?"* I said. *"I don't know, I just knew it, there is something different about you."* she answered. I smiled and thanked her, they introduced themselves to me and I did the same and they went outside to their car.

When I came out to put my first son in the van, I didn't notice them still sitting in their car in the parking lot. I then proceeded to go to the toddler building next door to get my older son and loaded him in the van also. As I was getting in, her husband jumped out of their car and asked me if he could talk to me for a moment. I was a little hesitant, but I stepped back out of the van to see what he wanted.

He began to ask me questions saying he had noticed that the van I was getting in said it was the Rescue Mission, was I staying there? I guess thinking back, most people would have been insulted, but I had left all my pretense far behind long before this conversation. I quietly explained that I had been in an abusive relationship, fled to Florida and ended up with nowhere to stay and how God had given me an open door at the Rescue Mission. I told him quickly of how much getting saved had changed my life and how things were already getting better. I had a new job and plan to get back on my feet soon.

He then asked me more questions. Did I get my G.I. Bill when I was in the military? Yes, I did. Do I have plans of going back to college? College money, also known as the GI Bill, is why I initially went in, but I explained how now that I have two children alone, my priority was to provide for them. I explained how maybe one day when they are older, maybe high school or college age, I will go back to school if I can't figure it out sooner. His questions seemed so extremely odd!

Then, he began to explain to me how they were also believers and how God really caused them to notice me and they didn't know why. Then when he came out and saw the Rescue Mission van, they couldn't pull away because they realized, I must be staying there. They began to explain to me how they were connected to a Scholarship Program for former military members that not only provided full tuition including books, but also gave you an apartment on extremely low subsidized rent.

He explained that it wasn't his decision who was selected to be in the program, how they were selective and although there were many people who apply that don't make it in the program that maybe I should apply. He believed this is why God had them wait for me to come back out, to share this opportunity with me. If I did apply and was accepted, with full tuition assistance and my books paid for, all I would have to worry about is my utilities and my low subsidized rent which my GI Bill would cover much of that. As he spoke to me, I felt the presence of God so strong, and as he explained the scholarship program, tears ran down my face. I knew this was the Lord Himself opening up yet another door for me! I had given up on my dreams for college and thought I'd resign to a "normal" life of just working to get by, but again, God had a better plan.

Ephesians 3:20 Now to him who is able to do immeasurably more than all we ask or imagine, according to his power that is at work within us

Of course you know that God did open that door! I was chosen to be a recipient of the scholarship and to be a member of the program. So only a little more than three months after I had moved into the Rescue Mission and the Lord spoke to me as I laid on the cold, hard floor that night, I was moving into my own three bedroom apartment with a full scholarship to return to college! I know to many an apartment is not something to get excited about. However when you've gone from driving half way across the country with two infants in a Toyota Tercel with only $200, to living in a small abandoned children's bedroom in the house of people who don't want you there, to living in a small room at a Rescue Mission, to receiving a three bedroom apartment from the hand of God! It may as well have been a mansion! To me, it was!

I remember the cold day in December when the guys I didn't know from the Scholarship Program came with a trailer to move me from the

Rescue Mission to the program's apartment complex. They were my fellow veterans, so we did have a camaraderie from our similar backgrounds. They introduced themselves and helped me as I moved out. The Rescue Mission had a policy that you could shop from their second hand thrift store and get all the furniture you needed for your apartment when you leave the program. The mattresses were those that other's had discarded when they got new ones, I remember searching through so many of them trying to find ones that didn't have stains on them. Finally I found a clean mattress, a couch, a chair, a small dining room table with a leg that wobbled and two mismatched chairs for the table. I also found a very old coffee table that had a huge knife hole in it, apparently someone had gotten angry who owned it previously and had put a large kitchen knife through the tabletop, but again, it was functional and that's all that mattered. The selection wasn't great, but I didn't mind. I was just so thankful to have a place to live for my children and me that we could finally call our own! I remember going to the dollar store to get a tablecloth and table runner to cover the knife whole in the coffee table. I had nothing needed to set up a home fully, but I was so thankful! As the men moved the second and maybe even third or fourth hand furniture in and I brought in my garbage bags full of our clothing, I couldn't help but continue to praise God out loud. When they left, I remember turning from the front door, hugging the wall and crying in thanksgiving to God! I am overwhelmed to the point of tears now as I type this, remembering how much it meant to me, that God was REAL, that He kept His Word and that He loved me like no one else had ever done. His Word in Matthew 6 had promised me, only eight months before that day that He would provide for me because I was His child and now here I was, after having risked so much, in my own place given to me by the hand of God Himself.

God blessed me simply because I chose to believe Him and take Him at His Word. The stories of that amazing season in my life go on and on. When I first moved in, I had no plates, no pans, nothing. I went to Dollar General and bought one very cheap saucepan, one frying pan of equal quality and some cheap washable plastic plates, bowls and cups. I got 2 of each so my 2-year-old son and I would have something to eat and drink from. I got a broom and dustpan, only the bare necessities needed.

I moved into my place at the beginning of December. I remember as Christmas approached, I honestly was just happy my kids were so young, because they wouldn't know to be disappointed about gifts. A Christmas tree and gifts was something I was not even thinking about getting but I hoped that next year I would be able to make it up to them. Once again, God had another plan. I got a phone call from the Rescue Mission and they said they had thought about me, knowing I had just moved out and wondered if they could bring some gifts for my children. When they arrived, there were so many gifts it was overwhelming! There was even a brand new bicycle for my two year old!

I had gotten a new job in November and there was a guy in our office that just seemed to really not like me. His bad treatment of me had just gotten him in trouble so around Christmas time he was very upset with me! I remember that day before the office closed down for Christmas break as we were all preparing to leave for the day, he rushed back in with a huge wrapped box, literally dropped it on my desk and yelled "here...Merry Christmas!" then abruptly turned around, stormed out and slammed the door! To be honest, his bad attitude made me want to put that gift right back on his desk and say thank you, but no thank you.

Then an older and wiser lady who also worked in our small office encouraged me to keep the gift and how God will use even your enemies to bless you when He decides to. As I opened it, I was amazed, it was a very expensive and very nice kitchen set. It had a dish set for eight with glasses, pots, pans and real silverware. The box was so heavy I couldn't carry it by myself! I had not told anyone I only had one pot, one pan and 2 plastic dishes, but God knew and He caused a man who hated me at the time to buy it for me!

Over the holiday break, because my new job was in a governmental agency type office, they shut down from Christmas until after New Year's Day. Because I was a new hourly employee, I hadn't earned any paid vacation days and so that two-week break was not paid for me.

I had just moved into my new apartment and had made an arrangement for my large electric deposit to be paid in two payments and the next one was coming up at the beginning of January. If

I missed that payment, they were going to turn off my lights immediately. Of course at this same time, my small, subsidized rent for January would also be due and I had no paycheck coming for the beginning of January.

I had made that last paycheck in mid-December last as long as I could and I was literally down to my last $7, just enough to buy my bus pass to return to work and school that following Monday. I had food for the week so I would be fine and I was just so thankful that by Friday I would have another paycheck coming, hoping the electric company would give me grace until then. I went to church that Sunday with my last $7 in my purse. I had already been a tither, but I hadn't yet learned about sacrificial giving, the concept was yet another that was new to me.

The pastor preached a powerful Word that day, and when it came time for the offering, I clearly heard the instruction of the Lord in my heart, to sow all the money I had. My heart began to pound as I thought about it, because this was literally all the money I had. It was only $7 and I needed this for my bus pass to get me to work and school, to get me the paycheck by Friday that I desperately needed!

Seven dollars was clearly not going to make much difference in the church's offering, but here I am, feeling that God is saying, "give it all!" It wasn't an easy thing to do mentally, but spiritually I knew that what I had was not enough to meet my need. I understood for the first time that I needed to sow sacrificially, to sow a precious seed. So I pulled out my $7 and whatever the last little bit of change was that was at the bottom of my purse, I put it in an envelope and I sowed it. As I rode the church bus home, the thoughts of "what in the world am I going to do?!" tried to creep up, but I resisted them and prayed quietly to Him.

When I got home, in a short time, my phone rang. It was one of my fellow female soldiers in the Scholarship Program that lived upstairs from me. She said she had noticed that I was catching the bus every day around the same time in the morning that she was driving to school. She said that since we both went to the same school, if I would like, she would be glad to start driving me to school. Wow, here were the first signs of provision already! I thankfully accepted her offer and now I knew how I would get to school. I used to catch the bus from school to my job in the afternoon so even though she gave me a ride to school that day, I had no idea how I was going to get to my job. Then the same thing happened at school! One of my classmates said he drove past my job on his way home from school and offered to give me a ride to work from school. When I got to my job, I was about 5-7 miles from my day care and apartment so worst case scenario I could walk but my new friend who had driven me to school, also offered to pick me up at work on her way home back to our apartment complex. I wouldn't miss one day of work or school even though I sowed my bus pass money! Then when I got home the second day of this new routine, on a Tuesday, my former pastor in California had sent me an overnight envelope in the mail. I had not told him I was in need of money, I had only contacted him and his wife to let them know where I was, that I was doing well, that God had been blessing and to give them my address to keep in touch. The letter he sent explained that on that Sunday at the end of his service in California, which due to the time difference would have been only hours after I had sown my sacrificial seed here in Orlando, the Lord spoke to him and told him to do a second offering for me and to overnight mail it to me.

He playfully told me that he was a little jealous of the response because more came in for me than did for the church budget that week! He concluded that it didn't matter to him though, because he knew he heard from God and so he was obeying to get it to me. There was more money in that overnight envelope than I would have made in those two weeks I was unable to work. As I read the letter he closed with this: "*P.S. – Weeping may endure for a night, but joy comes in the morning!*" I literally screamed out loud and began to cry and praise God. There was enough to pay my electric deposit off, my rent and buy groceries and a bus pass and still have some left over! The moment I sowed my $7 seed, God released His instructions to my former pastor all the way on the other side of the country to provide an immediate harvest!

The point to sharing all of this in depth detail with you is to encourage you to believe God! The principles of having faith in Him and trusting Him to provide for you are not something I had to learn at the risk of not having enough to eat out or get my nails or hair done. Those were things I could not afford to indulge in back then. I had to learn the principles of hoping in Him at the risk of what felt like my very life. His principles were all that stood between death and me at times. His principles were all that stood between homelessness and me. There's something about just having come out of that situation that makes the threat of going back so real. While the threat was real, His Word and His power were even more real!

The real blessing He gave me was this new life that included a hunger to serve Him and obey the life principles in His Word. At this time in my life that I experienced all His blessings as I described to you in this chapter, I honestly still didn't know hardly any of the church rules for living. I was only going by what I received from Him in my studies, prayer time and also at church through the preaching. He dealt with re-wiring my heart about life! Not about clothing style or even about church doctrine. He taught me how to see life and how to live life, to forgive and love people as He did, to have a great work ethic and do all I did as unto Him, and so much more! As I obeyed His Word and the promptings of His Spirit, He led me through the wilderness season of my life and blessed my life in the midst of the wilderness! The week after I experienced that miraculous blessing as a result of sowing sacrificially in obedience to His voice, my next life-changing miracle was about to happen.

The Scholarship Program required me to do 20 hours of month of community service time through their established tutoring programs. I picked a local elementary school because it was close to our apartment and I could walk there.

When I walked into the cafeteria that same first week of January, I was clearly the new kid on the block. I was introduced to all the other soldiers who were volunteering at that school as part of the program. There was one guy who stood out to me; turned out he was new also, just arrived fresh from serving overseas. I remember thinking I was going to stay far away from him because the last thing I needed was a man in my life, or so I thought. Once again, God had other plans.

First we were assigned to the same group of 1st graders to tutor. Then, because I had no family or friends in the area, I always brought my children with me everywhere I went, so my two-year-old son had a new favorite friend and it was this same guy. Every time I turned around, my son was with him, running after him, coloring and showing him the pictures and just generally talking his ear off. I remember apologizing to him for my son bothering him. As I was about to make my son leave him alone and sit down with me, he refused and said he didn't mind him at all. He said he was his little buddy and he was no bother at all. Some nerve this guy had, to be cute and nice too! Yes, I thought, I must DEFINITELY stay away from him!

The second week of January came up and we were taking all the children being mentored by the Scholarship program to the Martin Luther King Day parade in downtown Orlando. A girlfriend and I were discussing what we were going to do for the Valentine's Day holiday coming up and I made the mistake of saying out loud that I had no one to spend it with and he overheard me. From that moment on, he began to pursue me and literally went everywhere I did. I was most definitely flattered and really did love his personality and his drive for his future. However, after having been through so much trauma in my former relationship, being single to me, was a huge gift, one that I was very thankful for and that I was afraid to even think about giving up. I liked him very much but I was so afraid of repeating the mistakes of my past.

As he continued to follow me around, we were spending a lot of time together and I knew I was starting to like him very much also. In complete fear, I began to cry out to God one night and then I read for the first time the book of Ruth. I honestly didn't originally see any correlation, as I was just doing my normal studying and it was just my time to read the book of Ruth. I loved the story and as I got to the place where Boaz redeemed Ruth, I heard the voice of God tell me not to be afraid and that this young man was my "kinsman redeemer." As I continued to cry out to Him, because although I heard Him speak, in this area, I was very afraid because of my past experience, He took me to 1 John 4 and let me know that because I was in His love, I had nothing to fear.

1 John 4:18 There is no fear in love. But perfect love drives out fear, because fear has to do with punishment. The one who fears is not made perfect in love.

I made the difficult decision to trust God to lead me in who I was to be in relationship with, which may have been harder for me than believing against all those bad circumstances for provision. He told me to trust Him and that is exactly what I did. I was free now, by His love, to love another man as my husband. Within a few weeks, he proposed to me and eight months later we were married.

Before we were married we faced some very tough situations as a couple. There were major obstacles in our way trying to prevent our marriage. As we were praying and seeking God during those tough situations, there was one specific night where everything turned for us and has impacted our lives to this day also.

As we kneeled together to pray, we released our upcoming wedding to the Lord and we made a commitment together that if He saw us through the opposition that we would serve Him with our marriage all the days of our lives. From the moment we saw breakthrough and were married, it was as if we were on a rocket and the fuse was

SAMANTHA M. PHILLIPS

lit the moment we said I do. Within three months he was asked to preach his first sermon and within three years, we were sent out to pastor a church in a neighboring community.

We were only in our mid-twenties and were already pastors. There are others we know who are or were senior pastors in their twenties. All of them, were men and women who grew up in church, and all of them were child preachers, most of them starting before their teen years. They were groomed their entire lives to be pastors.

My husband and I on the other hand both came from troubled inner city pasts, had a long list of past issues neither of us were proud of and neither one of us felt prepared or qualified to lead God's people in a role as important as a Senior Pastor. Despite not being prepared or qualified in

118

the eyes of men, God chose to use us and we've been blessed to see God do great things through ministry.

Now some 13 years later at the time of this writing, we've experienced some amazing things in living life for God. We are the thankful parents of SIX wonderful children, four boys and twin girls. Over the years, as we've obeyed the voice of God and His Word, He has blessed our lives beyond what we could have even asked for or dreamed of! We humbly live in the best, ride in the best, wear the best, eat the best and go first class in life!

We've travelled the World and enjoyed our family and each other every single year of this journey. Every desire of my heart, as I've trusted

God with it, and served Him with my life, He has truly provided.

His Word is true! You can trust God! God's greatest desire is to be loved and trusted! Because He loves you so much when you decide to love and trust Him, there is no limit to how much He will bless you. As I once heard the great Bishop I.V. Hilliard say "God will fill any bag you give Him!" when your desire is to please Him! When you have faith for something and trust Him for it, according to His purpose, you are giving Him a bag to fill. He is always faithful to fill the bags you give Him! Again I say, you CAN trust God!

THE CONCLUSION OF THE MATTER

As you've read this book with the many stories and testimonies of the beginnings of my walk in faith serving God, I pray that He has touched your heart to know that His love is very real and He is very much concerned about your life and your purpose. If you are in an abusive situation or if you were once abused and are still being held captive by unforgiveness or fear, I pray that you will see clearly for yourself that God is a deliverer! You CAN trust God! No matter what your station is in life, no matter the situation, faith in Jesus Christ is not a "religion" thing, it's a real life, relationship with your Creator!

I knew nothing of religion and He blessed me through relationship. Over the years I learned about religion and I have yet to see anything productive come from it. Real relationship has produced miraculous results not only in my life but also in the countless lives of others just like me. I encourage you, man or woman, adult or child, by faith in Jesus Christ, you can overcome all the negative circumstances and situations in life in a very real and eternal way.

(KJV) 2 Corinthians 4:8We are troubled on every side, yet not distressed; we are perplexed, but not in despair; 9Persecuted, but not forsaken; cast down, but not destroyed;

CPSIA information can be obtained at www.ICGtesting.com
Printed in the USA
LVOW06s2312290815

451988LV00007B/17/P